THE
ULTIMATE
MARRIAGE
VOW

THE
ULTIMATE
MARRIAGE
VOW

21 DAYS TO A LIFELONG COMMITMENT

NYT Best-Selling Author
DARLENE SCHACHT

Time-Warp Wife Ministries

The Ultimate Marriage Vow:
21 Days to a Life-Long Commitment

Time-Warp Wife Ministries
Winnipeg, Manitoba

Copyright © 2022 by Darlene Schacht
ISBN 978-1-988984-14-8

Cover design by Darlene Schacht

TABLE OF CONTENTS

Introduction

Growing up, my dad was fondly known as "Andy the Handyman." He fixed our toys, unclogged drains, and mended our purses. He even stretched our shoes when we needed him to!

I'll never forget his red toolbox. It's almost as though it was a part of him, the way mom's purse was a part of her. Whether he was travelling to and from home, or just tinkering around the house, he carried it often. Pulling out one tool for this, and another for that, he kept our home safe and secure.

If it was broken, we took it to dad and he fixed it. When mom's pot needed a new handle, he replaced it with a wooden spool. The broken rolling pin got a new dowel, and way back in the day he made a bedroom door from a cardboard box. If something was torn, Mom would mend it. If a button popped off, she would fix it.

Money was scarce for a while, and so they learned to value the things that they owned. Clothes were passed down from one girl to the next, and if it wasn't in style we took it to our sewing machines for a few alterations. Being the youngest, it's no wonder I sewed as much as I did.

Watching the Carol Burnett show with light bulbs in hand, we darned socks. Yes: with a light bulb, a needle, and thread.

If it was broken, we fixed it. That was our motto.

It was comforting to see the way they cared for our home, but more importantly the way that they cared for each other.

During those formative years we learned the importance of commitment and stewardship. We learned that a vow was a vow.

During the good times and bad, they exercised patience, forgiveness, and grace. Sure, there were days like anyone else when the going was tough, but giving up wasn't an option. They worked together to work things out and weathered each storm that blew through.

Mom and Dad held onto the promise, "Till death do us part," and during that moment of silence when he took his last breath, they were still holding on to each other.

It's a Thousand Little Things

"I do," is one of the shortest sentences in the English language and yet it carries a promise too vast to be measured by man. It's not one thing we do, but a thousand little things that make up the sum of our vows.

Long-lasting love doesn't happen by accident. We don't find ourselves holding hands after twenty-five years with the one that we love by pure chance. Love is deliberate, intentional, purposeful, and, in the end, worth every minute that we give of ourselves to another.

It's giving up your right to be *right* in the heat of an argument. It's forgiving another when they let you down. It's loving someone enough to step down so they can shine. It's friendship. It's being a cheerleader and trusted confidant. It's a place of forgiveness that welcomes one home, and arms they can run to in the midst of a storm. It's grace.

It's giving of yourself tirelessly down paths you'd never imagine to travel. Through sickness and pain, poverty and loss, it's carrying the weight of another. It's being the smile they see in the morning, and the body they hold close at night. It's pure love. It's standing together in the face of adversity. It's riding alongside each other in a battle that threatens to tear down your marriage and seeks to grab hold of your faith. It's strength under pressure.

It's listening to the heart of another and understanding their pain. It's offering words of encouragement when they need it most. It's walking hand-in-hand in the park, and a gentle kiss in the pouring rain. It's laughing together.

It's endless compassion.

Marriage is ordained by the almighty God, and when we live out our vows according to His incredible wisdom and grace, love never fails.

A Christ-Centered Marriage

The way that we choose to embark on this journey will set the course for our lives. Will we choose God's plan for marriage which is perfect in every way? Or do we consider His ways too old-fashioned or old-school for couples today?

Here's the thing. The Bible tells us that He's the same God yesterday today and forever. He's both the author and finisher of our faith. And the idea of marriage? It was planned long before any of us stepped foot on this earth.

We serve an incomparable God who is perfect in every way and Whose wisdom runs deeper than any one of us could ever imagine.

God's Word is the perfect guidebook for marriage, and those who live by His Word will reap the blessings that obedience brings.

Will some of these vows look the same as the next person's marriage? Yes, on the outside they might. An encouraging wife could build up her husband and, yes, any couple could cultivate friendship. The difference however is that a Christ-centered marriage is an extension of our love toward God.

When we love God with all of our heart, we seek His will for our marriage. We don't love our husbands the way that we do because it's popular to do so, or because it's a family tradition. We do so because we believe that His Word is just as powerful and effective as it was thousands of years ago. We do so because His wisdom runs deep. And, we do so because we love God with all our heart, our soul and our mind. When the going gets tough, we lean on God's wisdom instead of our own.

Whether we're sitting in a church pew, we're down on our knees in prayer, or we're standing at the sink washing dishes, our marriage brings glory to God when we love because we love Him.

The Next 21 Days

The Ultimate Marriage Vow is a 21-day journey through love. It encourages us to cherish our vows, love our husbands, and seek God's plan for our marriages. We're all a work in progress, and regardless of how strong a marriage may be there's always room to grow. And so, I encourage you to enter with a heart that is willing to learn, and willing to yield to God's will.

Each day includes a vow and a challenge that's designed to strengthen one area of your relationship. Put aside 10 minutes every morning to read over a chapter and pray for your marriage.

At the close of each day, use the space provided at the end of the chapter labelled "Appreciate the Little Things" to jot down some appreciation, gratitude, or admiration. For example, you might want to record something that you appreciate about your husband: maybe there's something you're grateful for, or perhaps he went out of his way to do something special. Doing this exercise at the end of each day will help you to gain a deeper appreciation of the blessings at hand.

Will You Give Me 21 Days?

I'm a sleeper.

I'm especially known to nap in the car. Whether we're driving across town or halfway across the country, I sleep. For as long as I can remember, I've done this.

I also sleep on airplanes. In fact, two years ago I stepped onto a plane in Hershey Pennsylvania and woke up in Chicago. I opened my eyes asking myself, "Are we taking off, or have we arrived?" I had no idea if the ride was over or about to begin.

Maybe it's the steady hum of the motor that lulls me to sleep. Or could it be that I have full confidence in the driver? I tend to think it's a combination of both.

As I got to thinking about that today, I was reminded of my journey through faith and how I'm trusting in God to carry me through. Whether we realize it or not, we rely on the provision of God every day. We break a nail, it grows back. We scrape a knee, it heals. We take a breath, another one follows. The sun sets, and it rises. We plant seeds, and they grow... The more I trust in the Lord, the more I can rest in His strength.

God knew exactly what He was doing when He created this earth. Every part of creation, from the sky to the deepest parts of the sea is uniquely crafted and nurtured by Him.

We know that we can trust Him with that, but do we trust God when it comes to our marriage? Do we really believe that He's got a plan?

Never Say "Never"

Maybe you're a newlywed couple. You've just started this journey and it's all going well. You've married the man of your dreams, and so far, the idea of hardship and sorrow is out of mind. You can't imagine anything coming between you, let alone the problems that other couples have had. Perhaps you've said to yourself, "That would never happen to us." Maybe it won't, but don't fool yourself into thinking it *can't.*

Remember the words of Peter who earnestly vowed to stand by the Lord just hours before he denied Him, "Even if I have to die with you," he said, "I will never disown you." (Mark 14:31, NIV)

And what did the Lord say to Peter? "Simon, Simon, behold, Satan hath desired to have you, that he may sift you as wheat." (Luke 22:31, KJV)

If only Peter realized the gravity of those words, then maybe he would have spent the night praying instead of falling asleep. Perhaps he would have been prepared to face the enemy instead of cowering behind his denial.

Don't wait until the enemy knocks on your door to suit up for battle. Do what it takes to strengthen your marriage today, so that you will be ready tomorrow.

The first step in defending your marriage is accepting the fact that a battle is raging and Satan is after your soul. If he could put a chink in Peter's armour, imagine the damage he can do to your marriage.

The second step is preparing yourself for attack by strengthening the bond of your marriage, praying for your marriage, and digging into God's Word. The more we're absorbed in His Word, the more we walk in His will. The more we walk in His will, the more we're transformed into the wife He designed us to be.

He Holds the Power of Life and Death

Maybe you've been married for a while, and maybe some days you just want to give up. You wonder if there's any use in trying, because you've both failed in the past. And, maybe you think to yourself, "This marriage is long past saving. There's no way it can work."

Turning to the scriptures, I read Ezekiel 37:1-14, and I know without a shadow of a doubt that God is sovereign. He holds the power of life and death in His hands. Nothing is too difficult for Him!

God gives Ezekiel a vision. He is sent down to the valley of bones. The Bible refers to them as "dry bones." In other words, they were way past dead.

God asked Ezekiel, "Can these bones live?"

His answer? "Oh Lord God, thou knowest."

Are you ready to say the same thing, or do you doubt the power of God? In other words, do you have more faith in your problems or in God's ability to solve them?

The vision goes on to show Ezekiel how they came to life. They rose to their feet. They were an extraordinary army. And, listen to this:

"Then you, my people, will know that I am the LORD, when I open your graves and bring you up from them. I will put my Spirit in you and you will live, and I

will settle you in your own land. Then you will know that I the LORD have spoken, and I have done it, declares the LORD." (Ezekiel 37:13-14, NIV)

Ezekiel's Valley of Dry Bones serves to teach us an important lesson, which is that God specializes in miracles. He replaces the stench of death with life. He gives hope where all hope is lost. He wants to breathe life into your marriage. The same faithful God who brought you this far can bring you much further yet, but the question is: are you willing and ready to trust Him?

Remember the Israelites who were hemmed in with their back against the Red Sea. Remember the Egyptian army with over 600 chariots that were marching toward them. Remember how terrified they were when they cried out to the Lord, but (most importantly) remember His mighty power and strength. Remember how the Red Sea was divided and how He saved them that day. Remember that He's the same God we serve.

How often do I miss those opportunities to simply wait and be still? How often do I put God in a box because I don't understand?

The sick are made whole, a blind man can see, the dead come to life… and you wonder if your problems are too big for God.

Will You Give Me 21 Days?

Corrie Ten Boom once wrote, "When a train goes through a tunnel and it gets dark, you don't throw away the ticket and jump off. You sit still and trust the engineer."

How many times have couples jumped ship? Looking at the divorce rates in Canada and the US, the answer is a disappointing "far too often." Too many couples have given up before they had a chance to experience what a mature relationship has to offer. Too many couples give up. They part ways before they experience the joy of growing together God's way.

I've been there. I've smelled the stench of death in my own marriage. We've been to rock bottom where all hope was seemingly lost. But that wasn't the end—something incredible happened when we surrendered our marriage to God. Winter turned to Spring, Spring turned into Summer, and here we are decades later thanking God for His life-saving grace.

Those who trust God are wise to remember that He's at work in their life. Whether we understand it or not, whether we're overwhelmed, stressed out, or at the end of our rope, we can always rest in His power.

Every difficult day and every trial we face, is an opportunity to connect with God in ways we might otherwise miss. And when we do trust in God? We open a door to deliverance, mercy, and grace.

And so, I'm asking, will you give me 21 days? That's all I'm asking you for—3 weeks, 10 minutes a day, and a gentle heart that's willing to yield. Give me 21 days to show you what God can do for your marriage. 21 days to remind you that marriage is a gift worth fighting for. 21 days to love on and pray for your husband. 21 days to a life filled with love, joy, and peace. 21 days to a life-long commitment.

Teach Me to Love, Lord

I woke up today with love on my mind, and a burden to love in my heart. I guess you could say it's been a while coming, but today even more so.

"Teach me to love, Lord," I said, "Teach me what it means to love and be loved."

I thought of all of the people in my life: the good, the bad, the close and the distant… How each one deserves compassion, kindness, a smile, and some grace.

I was reminded that hurt people hurt, and therefore to love those who hurt. For it's only in loving them that I begin to understand them. And when I understand them–that's when I love.

I thought about the days that are good and the ones that are seemingly bad. How the difficult days serve to teach and to strengthen my faith. I asked God to teach me to love and embrace each day as it comes, whatever may come.

I thought about the beauty of contentment. How some love the little they have, while others only hunger for more.

Teach me to love, Lord. Teach me the art of contentment.

I thought about the divisions and disagreements I've seen in the church, and with that I see a need to love all the more. For it's in loving that we open our hearts to communication, healing, and unification.

I thought about the changing seasons. How I love the summer sunshine and despise the cold of winter. I asked the Lord to teach me how to embrace the beauty of freshly fallen snow, the warmth of hot chocolate on cold and windy nights, and the joy of playing games around the table with our kids.

I thought about the beauty of my youth and the fear of growing old, and I asked the Lord to teach me how to love.

May He give me the courage to face the days ahead and to love the person I become. To cherish the wisdom that comes with growing old. To embrace the lines upon my face that a lifetime of smiles left behind, and to recognize the beauty emerging from within.

Teach me to love, Lord. Teach me to love.

Before you begin this journey, stop to pray. Ask the Lord to teach you what it means to love and be loved. Ask Him to help you get through the difficult days, and to find joy in the trials you face. Ask Him to open your heart, to strengthen your faith, and to bless your marriage as only He can.

DAY
1

To Be a Constant Friend & Companion

*A man that hath friends must shew himself friendly:
and there is a friend that sticketh closer than a brother.*

Proverbs 18:24, KJV

As we embark on this 21-day journey, I'd like to go back to the place where it all began for each one of us. The days before "we," when it was just "you" and "he." Back to the foundation of friendship where a seed of romance was planted and watered until it took root.

Remember those days? What was it like to be new-found friends? How was life different?

Michael and I were friends for several months before we dated. Inseparable, like two peas in a pod, side-by-side day in and day out. We spent hours on end talking on the phone about the music we liked, the movies that made us cry, friends from the past... More than anything else, we had fun.

We went for picnics, attended church, and spent time at the park. Taking long walks, I'd feel the brush of his hand against mine wondering when and if they'd ever connect.

Like any new and exciting friendship, I was sincerely interested in knowing what he was about, and so I asked questions and listened intently to every word that he spoke and every story he told.

There was no doubt in my mind that this man was my very best friend. We made every effort to spend time together.

Fast forward about 15 years. Michael and I were struggling with the day to day details of starting a new business. We were dealing with the loss of five babies to miscarriage, and had started raising a family. Michael was working long hours and I was busy at home taking care of the kids.

Unfortunately, like many couples who are busy being "Mom and Dad," our friendship was swept to the side for a time. Thankfully, we've put in the effort to pull friendship back to the forefront of our relationship.

If you're wondering what that looks like, it's a matter of carving out time to spend in each other's company, and enjoying the time that you have. Alone time? That's good, but not always practical when you have a house full of kids. Spending time with your husband might be putting a puzzle together at the kitchen table, watching a "Lord of the Rings" marathon (which I recently did), or enjoying a picnic with your kids at the park.

Spend Time, Not Money

As much as I want to suggest "date nights" to you, I'm going to veer in a slightly different direction by sharing two romantic little nuggets with you.

IF WE HOPE TO REAP A GENEROUS HARVEST, WE HAVE TO PLANT SEEDS IN THE SOIL OF FRIENDSHIP.

The first one is this: my parents were married for over 60 years, and I don't ever remember them going out on a "date." It just wasn't their thing. They had a big family and they were careful about the way that they spent their money.

But here's what I did notice about them: aside from watching TV and gardening together, they spent time laughing together.

Looking back at it now, one of the things I loved most about spending time at the cabin was the fact that the walls were thin enough to hear Mom and Dad chatting and laughing in bed. Even on the most stressful of days, they would giggle and talk for a good half hour before falling asleep.

This afternoon I had lunch with a couple that's been happily married for 32 years. Do you want to know how they spend their evenings together? He reads classic novels to her while she works in the kitchen.

Plant Seeds in the Soil of Friendship

I asked Faith, "How many books has he read to you?"

"Hmm," she said scratching her head, "let me think. How long have we been married?"

My heart just about melted when I realized the countless hours they spent together cultivating a friendship over something as simple as reading a book.

Date nights don't get much better than that, do they?

If we hope to reap a generous harvest, we have to plant seeds in the soil of friendship. A pouring out of unselfish love, unconditional grace, unending support.

Take the opportunity to cultivate friendship within the walls of your home. Spend time, not money with the one that you love. Be willing to give up your time and attention. Be willing to give of yourself.

Today's Marriage Vow
To Be a Constant Friend & Companion

Today's Challenge
Carve out time in your day to cultivate friendship.

Appreciate the Little Things

_____

_____

_____

_____

_____

_____

_____

_____

_____

_____

_____

_____

Dear Heavenly Father,

I want to be a good friend and companion. I want to be the woman my husband longs to come home to. I want to hold his hand when we're old and laugh when our hair's turning grey.

I want to be by his side as we experience life. Facing our struggles together, lifting each up should we fall. And so, I'm asking for your guidance in this area of our marriage, Lord.

Teach us to be faithful friends who spend time together, and make time for each other. When life gets busy, remind us to keep our marriage alive by praying for each other and patiently offering grace.

Help us get back to the basics of being good friends. To hold on to our joy, and to recapture any we've lost.

Help me to be the wife You designed me to be.

In the name of Jesus, I pray. Amen.

DAY
2

To Choose Grace

One who loves a pure heart and who speaks with
Grace will have the king for a friend.

Proverbs 22:11, NIV

My husband had a brilliant idea. Can you sense a note of sarcasm there? I hope so, because there's definitely a wee hint of one. Anyway, my wonderful, always-resourceful husband decided to use our clothes closet for a podcast recording studio.

In all fairness to him, I have to admit that the acoustics are great in the closet. In all fairness to me, however, it's a little bit cramped when I'm looking for clothes.

With the new addition to the closet, I decided to clean it out this past weekend, and so I went through some old purses and packed up some of those too-tight clothes that have been hanging around.

WE HAVE TO LET GO OF SIN IF WE EVER HOPE TO GROW INTO THE IMAGE OF CHRIST.

More of You, Lord. Less of Me

As I got to purging my junk, I was reminded of an old saying from Smith Wigglesworth, "More of you, Lord. Less of me." It's a small statement, and yet those words are life-changing.

You can't fill a drawer that's jam-packed with garbage any more than God can fill a life that's jam-packed with sin. We have to let go of sin if we ever hope to grow into the image of Christ.

Every day we're faced with decisions that call us to lay down our sin and pick up our cross. And each time we do, we're growing in grace.

Does He Deserve Grace?

If you're not familiar with the movie "The War Room," I urge you to sit down and watch it tonight. It's a powerful reminder to love with compassionate grace.

For those of you who are familiar with the movie, I want to bring you back to the scene where Miss Clara sits down in the living room with Elizabeth. Elizabeth hands over a long list of grievances she has with her husband—three pages in fact.

"You'll get the gist of it, when you read it," she says, passing the list to Miss Clara.

Without skipping a beat, Miss Clara poses a question, "Actually, I'm not gonna read it." She says, "My question to you is this: in light of all of these wrongs, does God still love Tony?"

After Elizabeth points out that her love for Tony is buried under a lot of frustration, Miss Clara replies, "So, he needs grace."

"I don't know if he *deserves* grace," Elizabeth sighs.

"Do *you* deserve grace?" Miss Clara asks.

And with that, I'm convicted. I'm reminded of all the times I've shortchanged Michael's character because he didn't measure up to my expectations. The days when I've been more frustrated with him than loving him like I should. Those times when I should have extended God's compassion and grace.

He gave up His life for us while we were yet sinners. And what did He say about those who whipped Him, spat in His face, and crucified Him?

"Father, forgive them, for they know not what they do."

It's that kind of grace that speaks volumes. And the same kind of grace that we need to put into action if we hope to grow in the image of Christ.

When we look at our husbands, what do we see? A caring compassionate man who struggles against temptation? Or are we too focused on his flaws to see anything else?

Do we see a man who leaves his socks on the floor or a man who takes his kids to the park after a long day at work?

Do we see a man who watches too much TV, or a man who works hard for his family?

Whatever we focus on are the thoughts that will grow. They can either be thoughts of adoration or bouts of frustration, but let me assure you whichever you choose will certainly grow.

It's Never Too Late to Choose Grace

It's never too late to change the course of your marriage, and it's never too late to choose grace. No, we can't change the past or wish away the things that we've done, but thanks to God's grace we can do better today.

Maybe you've said things you shouldn't have, and maybe he's done the same. But here's the good news in all of this—while the repercussions of sin may cut deep, God's sustaining grace leads to beauty and newness of life. God specializes in miracles. He replaces the stench of death with life. He gives hope where all hope is lost.

Today's Marriage Vow
To Choose Grace

Today's Challenge
Keep negative thoughts in check by reminding yourself that
we're all human saved only by the grace of God.

Appreciate the Little Things

_____

_____

_____

_____

_____

_____

_____

_____

_____

_____

Dear Heavenly Father,

A wise woman takes control of her anger and gives it over to You, but a foolish woman lets her anger control her. She entertains it, and invites it to stay. I don't want to be that woman, Lord. I want to be more like You.

I'm not perfect. I'm bound to hurt him and say things that sting, and so I need Your mercy and strength. I need Your Spirit to guide and to teach me to be a woman of compassion and strength.

Help me to understand my husband, and to view him through a veil of grace. If we let each other down, may we also be the hand that picks each other up.

Teach me to examine my heart and to calm myself down when I need to. Give me the strength to control my anger before it controls me.

In the name of Jesus, I pray. Amen.

To Cherish This Gift

If the owner of the house had known at what time of night the thief was coming, he would have kept watch and would not have let his house be broken into. So you also must be ready, because the Son of Man will come at an hour when you do not expect him.

Matthew 24:43-44, NIV

I'll never forget that doll I once had. Peewee was smaller than most dolls her age, with blue eyes and blond hair that captured my heart. She was the greatest gift a young girl could have, and I knew that I loved her from the very first moment I unwrapped the box.

While the older kids were at school, I was busy at home with my Peewee–changing her diaper, washing her hair, and swaddling her wee little frame in a tea-towel blanket. At five-years-old, I was the best mom I could be.

By the time I was 8 we were closer than ever, but things around me were changing too fast. My sisters were getting married, having babies, and buying homes of their own. With that, mom suggested it might be time to let go—to let my niece have the doll since she was younger than me.

"You're a big girl." Mom said, "And besides that, you can play with the doll when you go over to visit."

I reluctantly agreed.

About a week later, we drove to their house. The closer we were, the more excited I was. I wanted to hold her, to play with her, and possibly try to convince them to give Peewee back.

Hustling out of the car, I ran through the gate and into the yard. Grass clippings littered the sidewalk, while something more frightening littered the grass.

Could it be? I wondered. Could that be my doll?

Stepping in for a closer look I saw something I'll never forget. Torn to shreds by the lawnmower, my doll was in pieces all over the grass.

What Will He Find When He Returns?

As I got to thinking about that today, I was reminded of the precious gifts we've been given from God. Our children, our families, our friends, and of course marriage—a gift of love we unwrap every day. We're given these gifts with a mission, to care for them in the best way we know how.

How are we caring for them? For our husbands? Our marriage? Do we cherish the husband we have? Are we treating him with due care?

WE'RE GIVEN THESE GIFTS WITH A MISSION, TO CARE FOR THEM IN THE BEST WAY WE KNOW HOW.

What will God find when He comes back for His church? A marriage that's thriving, or one that's neglected and tossed to the side? Can you say that you've been the best wife you know how? Or are you ashamed of the way that you've lived?

The good news in all this is that we have time to prepare. How much? We don't know. It could be a day, it could be year, but in any case, we've been given this time to make the most of our gifts.

Give Thanks With Your Life

When my kids give me a gift, I use it. If they make me a meal, I eat it. If they buy me a sweater, I wear it. I know that if it brings me joy, it brings them joy.

I'm reminded of my sister Bonnie, who is great at receiving gifts. It seems like every gift she gets is treasured dearly. From the minute she opens the box, you sense her deep appreciation and experience her joy.

The Lord, on the other hand, is the best giver. From the rising of the sun to the moment our head hits the pillow at night, and on through the night, He gives. We're surrounded by love and showered with gifts from on high, but the question remains, *do you delight in those gifts?* Do you stop to give thanks for our marriage? Do you find joy in being a wife?

You see, it's one thing to receive a gift from the Lord. It's another thing to take pleasure in that gift, to really see the gift for what it is, and to appreciate the giver.

R.C. Sproul once said, "God doesn't want us to just feel gratitude, but for us to show it by giving thanks to God with our lives."

We have the opportunity to do that. We can wisely invest in our marriage and glorify God by being the best wife we can be.

Today's Marriage Vow
To Cherish This Gift

Today's Challenge

Ask yourself how you would feel if Jesus returned today.
Is there anything you would change? If so, start
changing those things today.

Appreciate the Little Things

_____

_____

_____

_____

_____

_____

_____

_____

_____

_____

_____

Dear Heavenly Father,

Thank you for our home and everything in it. Thank you for this gift of marriage and a husband that I can share it with. Thank you for the leading of Your Holy Spirit who searches my heart and teaches me to love.

You've given me time to be the wife You have called me to be. You've given me direction, grace, understanding, and love. Don't let me waste a single minute of this time as I'm learning to grow.

I want to be a faithful servant who is ready for the return of the Master. I want to follow Your lead, as You continue to teach me and lead me through life.

Remind me to give thanks often, to complain *less* often, and to take pleasure in this life that we share.

In the name of Jesus, I pray. Amen.

DAY

4

To Seek the Will of the Lord

But seek first his kingdom and his righteousness,
and all these things will be given to you as well.

Matthew 6:33, NIV

I love it when Michael walks through the door and straight into my arms. I love a kiss on the forehead and a heart-warming embrace by the sink. I love the way he tucks in my blankets when I'm not feeling well. I love the attentive way that he shows me he cares.

We all want a sense of comfort and care, but the problem is that it's not always there. So, where does that leave us? What do we do? If our husbands aren't fulfilling our needs, then who or what is?

Remember the story of the Samaritan woman who came to the well to draw water? It's found in John Chapter 4. While the disciples were out grocery shopping (yeah, they were grocery shopping—check it out), Jesus met a woman at the well and asked her for a drink. He knew that this particular woman had a void inside her that led her to thirst for something more in her life. Like many of us, it moved her to return to the same proverbial well time and again hoping to fill that space that only Jesus could fill.

THE RECIPE FOR A GOOD MARRIAGE INCLUDES MORE THAN A FEEL-GOOD VIBE.

One by one, her five marriages failed. And like so many women today she was empty, discouraged, and searching for more.

Ruth Bell Graham writes, "It is a foolish woman who expects her husband to be to her that which only Jesus Christ Himself can be."

41

A bad marriage can feel like a spiritual vacuum at times, since weak relationships create that constant need to be filled. But here's the thing, even the strongest relationships can leave us feeling empty. It's a great thing when you enter into a deeper relationship with Christ, not such a good thing when we run into the arms of a stranger.

The best thing you can do for both your soul and your marriage is to fill that void with the thirst-quenching Spirit of God.

More of you, Lord—less of me.

The Beauty of Putting God First

C.S. Lewis once wrote, "In so far as I learn to love my earthly dearest at the expense of God and instead of God, I shall be moving towards the state in which I shall not love my earthly dearest at all. When first things are put first, second things are not suppressed but increased."

And so, you see, there's beauty in putting God first. It takes away every preconception of marriage, and it moves us to love as only God can teach us to love.

Be completely humble and gentle; be patient, bearing with one another in love. Make every effort to keep the unity of the Spirit through the bond of peace. (Ephesians 4:2-3, NIV)

Looking closer at that verse, I find a footnote in the Amplified Bible that reads, "The key to understanding this and other statements about love is to know that this love (the Greek word *agape*) is not so much a matter of emotion as it is of doing things for the benefit of another person, that is, having an unselfish concern for another and a willingness to seek the best for another."

All Love Comes from God

God doesn't give us these words for the sake of issuing rules. He gives them to us because He knows the recipe for a good marriage includes more than a feel-good vibe. He knows the benefits that come to those who humbly and patiently love, because He humbly and patiently loves.

Do you want more love in your marriage? Do you want joy and peace? Don't seek the fruit, seek the One from Whom the fruit grows.

But seek first his kingdom and his righteousness, and all these things will be given to you as well. (Matthew 6:33, NIV)

Those who seek to find love apart from their faith are like branches that long to bear fruit apart from the vine. When we abide in Christ and He in us, it's a natural extension of growing in grace.

A branch doesn't go looking for fruit. It soaks in the sun and the rain and, thus, fruit springs forth from within.

Right here and right now you have the opportunity for a better tomorrow. A chance to step aside and allow God to move in your marriage. But it has to start with seeking Him first.

Today's Marriage Vow
To Seek the Will of the Lord

Today's Challenge
Put God first in your marriage. Let every decision you make
flow through that funnel of faith.

Appreciate the Little Things

Dear Heavenly Father,

I'm choosing to serve. In serving You I know that I must turn my back on evil and walk away from temptation. I have to lay down my life to carry my cross.

Help me to put away distractions that keep me from serving You. Help me to recognize and confess my sin before it consumes me.

I've sinned. I've stumbled. I've taken my eyes off of You. And still, You call me Your servant and friend.

It's one thing to offer you lip service, it's another to live in sincerity and truth. Give me a pure heart and an earnest desire to walk in Your will.

Open my eyes to the opportunities around me, that I might be Your hands and feet in this world.

In the name of Jesus, I pray. Amen.

DAY
5

To Give Up My Need to Be Right

Do nothing out of selfish ambition or vain conceit. Rather, in
humility value others above yourselves, not looking to your
own interests but each of you to the interests of the others.

Philippians 2:3-4, NIV

I heard a story once about a woman who approached her pastor
before the morning service.

"I have a problem," she said. "I feel like I've lost my joy. I
don't fit in with the other women around me. I'm not good at

anything, really. I don't have a ministry, and come to think of it I don't have a purpose."

"Okay," he said, "we'll definitely talk more about this later. But I wondered if you could possibly do me a favor? I seemed to have dropped my wedding band some place. Would you take a quick look around the sanctuary for me?"

Knowing that he was recently widowed, Julie left his office determined to find the ring. She looked near the coats, she looked behind the copy machine, and before church started, she took a quick look around the sanctuary.

Resigned to the fact that it was nowhere in sight, she grabbed a seat at the back, laid her purse on the floor, and leaned in to listen. Just as she did, something shiny and bright caught her attention. It was the ring, laying under a chair, just two rows ahead.

At the end of the service, she met with the pastor again. "I found your ring!" she said, with a smile.

"Great," he said, "thank you! If you can stick around for a few minutes, I'd like to ask you about something."

When the crowd finally emptied the church, Julie and her family stood in the lobby with the pastor.

"Julie," he said, "how are you doing since we talked earlier this morning? Are you still feeling down?"

"Well," She said. "to be honest with you, I haven't had much time to think about it, I was too busy looking for the ring."

"Exactly," he said. "you see, the more we're concerned about others, the less we have time to worry about ourselves. Remember how I preached on the book of Philippians this morning, and how I pointed out that it's the most joyful book in the Bible? Well, smack dab in the middle of that joyful little book, Paul writes, 'Look not every man on his own things, but every man also on the things of others.' That's where you'll find your purpose, Julie. And that's where you'll find your joy!"

Love as He Loves

So, what does this mean in relation to marriage? Does it mean that we don't have a voice? Does it mean that we don't have the right to express our thoughts, our interests, our wants?

It just means that we should love as God loves. One who's empathetic, understanding, and kind. One Who was willing to step down to serve.

RATHER THAN CHOOSING OUR RIGHT TO BE RIGHT, WE NEED TO BE CHOOSING A PATH THAT IS RIGHT.

Have you ever pressed a coin into a ball of Play-Doh? What about your fingers? If the dough is pliable enough it takes on the likeness of the image. In fact, I've been able to see my fingerprints in the dough, almost as if it became one with my hand. That's what being empathetic and understanding is like: we welcome that impression upon our heart, carry each other's burdens, and take them to prayer. We listen intently hoping to learn, and we encourage each other to press on in faith.

It's Better to Do Right Than to Be Right

Communication is vital, and a healthy marriage is one where both a husband and wife have the opportunity to convey their thoughts with each other. Rather than choosing our right to be right, we need to be choosing a path that *is* right. Marriage isn't about winning or losing a fight. It's two people on the same team fighting for love.

The moment we realize that *doing* right is better than *being* right, we strengthen our marriage. You might have a point, and you may very well be correct, but hurting someone else to make that point isn't so cool.

A wife who values her husband higher than herself is willing to let go of her anger, gracefully drop out of a fight, and bring her frustration to prayer. Stepping back (by trying to diffuse an argument with kindness and love) and leaving it in the hands of the Lord, is taking a high road and should never be deemed as "losing a fight." Grace is undeserved favor. And while it might go unnoticed by your husband it doesn't go unnoticed by God.

Today's Marriage Vow
To Give Up My Need to Be Right

Today's Challenge

Let your voice be heard, but put down any weapons of
warfare. Practice holding your tongue when you're angry and
carrying your burdens to prayer.

Appreciate the Little Things

_____

_____

_____

_____

_____

_____

_____

_____

_____

_____

_____

Dear Heavenly Father,

Teach me to bridle my tongue, Lord. To bring it under subjection to Your Spirit so that I might speak wisely and well. Your Word tells me that sin doesn't end with the multiplying words, but the wise hold their tongue. And yet it's a lesson that's so hard to learn, as I live in a world that strives to have the last word and to prove themselves right.

Remind me often that it's more important to fight for my marriage than it is to fight to be right. Teach me to step back when I want to step up and be heard. Lead me as I seek to offer words of encouragement and grace. Help me to restrain myself when I'm feeling negative, and to weigh my thoughts before they come tumbling out.

Forgive me for all of the careless and thoughtless words that I've said. In the same way, help me to forgive and to extend grace to my husband.

In the name of Jesus, I pray. Amen.

DAY
6

To Honor You as the Head of Our Home

Now as the church submits to Christ, so also wives
should submit to their husbands in everything.
Husbands, love your wives, just as Christ loved
the church and gave himself up for her

Ephesians 5:24-25, NIV

Marriage, the way that God designed it to be, should reflect our relationship with Christ and submission to Him as our Lord. The Bible tells us that a man is to love his wife as Christ loved the church and gave Himself for it.

When we consider everything that Jesus did for us, only then can we see the responsibility that is placed on our husbands. A humble servant, who was willing to die for His bride.

They whipped Him, they spat in His face, they ridiculed Him, and, finally, they nailed Him to a cross. He came to serve and to die so that we might be saved.

Submission is a Powerful Choice

The Bible tells us that the husband is the head of the wife and that the wife should submit to her husband. With that, let's remember that submission is a powerful choice.

IT'S A MISSION WE CHOOSE, TO STEP DOWN AS WE YIELD OURSELVES TO GOD'S WILL.

It's not something that is, or should be, imposed upon us. It's a choice we make out of obedience to God, as everything we do stems from a love for the Lord and a decision to follow His will.

Looking at the covenant between Jesus Christ and the church, we see that the bride is under submission to a King Who gave himself for her.

It's a Mission We Choose

Let's not be confused. Submission is a beautiful word when it's in the right context. It stems from the word mission which means to release, to send, or let go. It's a mission we choose, to step down as we yield ourselves to God's will.

Jesus did both when He came to this world. He gave Himself up for His bride, and He lowered Himself in submission. A King who came to serve and to die taught us that equality isn't something we use to our own advantage.

Who, being in very nature God, did not consider equality with God something to be used to his own advantage; rather, he made himself nothing by taking the very nature of a servant, being made in human likeness. (Philippians 2:6-7, NIV)

Throughout the Bible, you'll see it said, "I would have obedience and not sacrifice."

Samuel said, Does the LORD delight in burnt offerings and sacrifices as much as in obeying the LORD? To obey is better than sacrifice and to heed is better than the fat of rams. (1 Sam. 15:22, NIV)

You see, it's easy to make a sacrifice to the Lord—but, to bring our lives under obedience to God—that's where the real challenge lies. We say that we love Him and serve Him, but are we willing to follow His will when it doesn't line up with ours?

Don't Let Expectations Get in the Way

The Jews rejected the authority of Jesus Christ as their Lord. It didn't make sense to them. Why would they hail a poor carpenter's son as their Lord? A child born in a manger? That was foolish to them. Their God—according to their expectations—would be a mighty warrior, not a lamb that was led to the slaughter. This expectation was the very thing that got in the way of their faith.

Don't let expectations or preconceptions get in the way of your faith. Scripture isn't a candy bowl by which we pick and choose our favorite words hoping to satiate our palette. It's a well-balanced diet of truth which, while difficult to swallow at times, brings nourishment to our soul.

My dad used to say, "God said it. I believe it. That settles it." And it should settle it: after all scripture isn't up for debate and pop-culture doesn't get a vote when it comes to my faith. Whether it makes sense to this world or not doesn't matter. I've decided to follow God's will in lieu of my own. It may seem foolish to some when I submit to my husband, but the foolishness of God is wiser than ours.

Does it mean that we're anything less? Absolutely not. And no, we're not any less precious to God.

When we submit to our husbands we substantiate the relationship between Christ and the church. We testify to the goodness and grace of our Savior. We show the world what it really means to love and give love.

Today's Marriage Vow
To Honor You as the Head of Our Home

Today's Challenge
While you honor your husband as the head of your home,
seek ways to encourage him in his role as a leader.

Appreciate the Little Things

_____

_____

_____

_____

_____

_____

_____

_____

_____

_____

Dear Heavenly Father,

In this modern, self-centered society, submission is a difficult truth for many to swallow. It goes against our natural desire to hold on to a sense of importance. It goes against our hope to be seen and be heard.

But Your wisdom runs deep, Lord. You teach me that it's more important to give than to get. You've shown me how submission is strength under control. You remind me of my importance in that You loved me so much that You sent Your Son to die so that I might have life.

Teach me to submit to my husband according to Your perfect will. Give me the strength to walk in truth even if the rest of the world doesn't choose to.

In the name of Jesus, I pray. Amen.

DAY
7

To Protect My Heart

Above all else, guard your heart,
for everything you do flows from it.
Proverbs 4:23, NIV

I've always been interested in taking care of my garden. In fact, I once said that I hoped there'd be at least some weeds in heaven because I enjoy gardening that much! If you drove down my street, there'd be no mistaking my house—I'm the one with the flower garden in the front yard. Make that plural.

I'm also the one with the cute little patio beside the front door. Up until about two years ago, I spent most of my free time outside. There was no place I felt closer to God than down on my knees in the dirt.

So, what happened two years ago? Well, let's just say that three years ago I put a stone patio in. Who knew that laying the bricks would be so tricky? There's a certain pattern that they have to be placed in if you want them to fit, and since I threw the little diagram away it was trial and error—actually more error than anything else.

After about four attempts at laying the stones, I finally got them to fit, and finished my patio up. It was beautiful, but there was one little problem: I didn't bend at the knees like I should have, and my back was feeling the pain.

Ever since then I've kind of lost my zeal when it comes to the garden. I don't feel like I'm 13 anymore when I'm playing in the mud. I feel more like I'm 85, and if I get down there I'm not sure that I'll be getting back up.

Last year was the worst year for my garden by far. I ignored it as much as I could and the back yard was nothing less than a mess. The weeds got so out of control that it took extra man-muscle to pull them all out.

Protect the Heart

What does any of this have to do with the heart? More specifically protecting my heart? A pure heart is a garden void of rocks and weeds. It's a heart unaffected by anger, resentment, and doubt. It's loving someone with only the best of intentions.

Those who value their marriage make every effort to protect the heart. They keep their thoughts in check, because they know that a garden with weeds has the potential to get out of control.

The fact that God is holy, pure, righteous, and good should be evident through the lives of His people. And if we're not reflecting the goodness of God, what message are we sending the world about who He is?

Scripture after scripture tells us to take our thoughts captive, to keep our bodies from sin, and to guard our hearts according to the Word. We all know that the smallest temptation can turn into sin and take root, when we allow it to seep in to our heart. Just one look, just one thought, just one email, just one day… And before you know it, you've broken your vows.

IF WE'RE NOT REFLECTING THE GOODNESS OF GOD, WHAT MESSAGE ARE WE SENDING THE WORLD?

Go to the Source

In one of his sermons, Charles Spurgeon shared a parable about a man from the East who came upon a mountain.

Looking down from the mountain, he saw the sun shining brightly on a river stream. It looked beautiful from afar, but as the old man made his way down the mountain, he soon discovered that the river was muddy and its water unfit to drink.

Nearby, he saw a young shepherd who sifted the water day after day, hoping to purify it enough to give to his flock.

Knowing that there was a better way, the wise man instructed the young boy to follow, and together they travelled for miles.

Finally arriving at the source of the stream, they found an open well, and sure enough it was flowing with water. Unfortunately, however, they also discovered that the animals which came to drink from the well were disturbing the soil around it. Because of these animals, the water was murky, muddy, and dark.

"My son," said the wise man. "Set to work now to protect the fountain and guard the well, which is the source of this stream. If you can keep these wild beasts and fouls away, the stream will flow pure and clear."

And so, while the young man went to work guarding the stream, the old man said, "My son if thou art wrong, seek not to correct thine outward life, but first seek to get thy heart correct. For out of it are the issues of life, and thy life shall be pure once thy heart is so."

Adapted from Spurgeon's Sermons Volume 02: 1856

Today's Marriage Vow
To Guard My Heart

Today's Challenge
Protect your marriage by guarding your heart.
Keep your thoughts in check, and weed out negativity.

Appreciate the Little Things

_____

_____

_____

_____

_____

_____

_____

_____

_____

_____

Dear Heavenly Father,

Your Word tells me "Whatever is true, whatever is noble, whatever is right, whatever is pure, whatever is lovely, whatever is admirable—if anything is excellent or praiseworthy—think about such things." And right after that, Your Word tells me to put these things into practice. And so, I'm asking that you would help us to practice these things in my marriage, Lord.

Help me to not only think on these things but to live them. Give me the strength to remain pure to my husband, and the virtue to be noble and true. Teach me ways to admire him and to build him up in healthy ways. Help me to bring out the best in him with the words that I speak, and the way that I love.

Remind me to keep my thoughts pure. To expect the best and to hope for the best in my husband.

In the name of Jesus, I pray. Amen.

DAY 8

To Pray for Our Marriage

Confess your faults one to another, and pray one for another, that ye may be healed. The effectual fervent prayer of a righteous man availeth much.

James 5:16, KJV

If you're anything like Michael and I, your wedding vows were beautiful. Sometimes I wonder if I was too distracted by the excitement of it all to realize just how wonderful they were. A promise to love, honor, and cherish each other. To laugh with him, to cry with him, and to take his hand in friendship. For better or worse, for richer, for poorer, in sickness and in health as long as we both shall live.

Words don't get much sweeter than those, do they?

The One Thing I'd Change

But if I could go back, and if we could do it all over again, I'd change one thing. I'd add one vow. I'd make a promise that would have changed the course of our marriage.

IN THE SAME WAY THAT A WOUND MIGHT BE PAINFUL AT TIMES WHEN A RIB IS REMOVED, SO WILL IT BE WHEN THE RIB HAS RETURNED.

That promise is this: *I solemnly swear to keep you in prayer each and every day of our lives as we surrender our marriage to God.*

Prayer is the most powerful force we can bring to our marriage, it's the greatest gift we can give to our spouse, and it's by far the best way to stay centered on Christ.

We Came from One Flesh

Marriage is a life-long process of growing together as one. But in the same way that a wound might be painful at times when a rib is removed, so will it be when the rib has returned. The Bible tells us,

And the two will become one flesh.' So they are no longer two, but one flesh. (Mark 10:8 NIV)

It's important to understand unity and to see the beauty of one flesh. We came from one body that we might again be that one body in a spiritual sense.

Although unity is a beautiful thing, it's not all that easy. Prayer must be an ever-present part of marriage if we hope to grow together as one, or more importantly to grow together in Christ.

Our Present Help in Trouble

We all have days when we struggle to—when we feel the sting of the rib. I can tell you from experience that it's a lot easier to be selfish than it is to sacrifice for the good of my marriage. But here's the thing–God doesn't call us to walk the easy road, He calls us to take up our cross and follow Him because He knows the joy and peace that comes to those who walk in obedience.

God is more than your ally. The Psalmist refers to Him as, "our refuge and strength, a very present help in trouble." (Psalm 46:1, NIV). Do you know what that says to me? That when we call upon the Lord, He doesn't simply show up for the rescue, He's already here.

Prayer is the most powerful force we can bring to our marriage, and the greatest gift we can give to our spouse. Don't let this treasure slip from your grasp.

I know, sometimes it seems like it's long past the point of repair. Some days it just feels impossible, and other days it feels even worse. But I also know that nothing is hopeless in the hands of our God. If we want to see change, we need to start believing in the power of God, and we need to be persistent in prayer.

Effectual Fervent Prayer

James 5:16 tells us, "The effectual fervent prayer of a righteous man availeth much."

Do you see that word, "fervent" in there? It tells me that a righteous woman is enthusiastic about prayer, and that her prayer life is something she values.

I used to ask my kids to check if the water was boiling on the stove. They'd often say, "I'm not sure. I see some bubbles coming up."

This was my answer to them, "When it's boiling, you'll know it's boiling. There's no mistaking it!"

Let's be that fervent when it comes to our prayer life. Let there be no mistaking the fact that you've brought your marriage to God and placed it at the foot of His throne. Get down on your knees if you want to, or stand up with your hands raised to God. Whatever you say, and however you pray, do it with all of your might! Pour yourself out to God and let His Spirit pour back into you.

Today's Marriage Vow
To Pray for Our Marriage

Today's Challenge

Take time every day to pray for your marriage, and if he's
willing, ask your husband to join you.

Appreciate the Little Things

_____

_____

_____

_____

_____

_____

_____

_____

_____

_____

Dear Heavenly Father,

Thank You for this incredible opportunity that I have to kneel in Your presence. Thank you for the honor and the privilege of prayer. May there never be a day that I cease to bow my head and give thanks for Your grace.

I'm bringing my marriage before You today, and laying it down at Your feet. I'm asking that You would mold and shape us into the couple You want us to be.

I ask that You lead me toward a stronger prayer life, as I bring my marriage before You each day. Help me to implement and strengthen this habit, Lord. Light a fire within me, and a passion to pray.

In the name of Jesus, we pray. Amen.

DAY
9

To Protect Your Reputation

Do not let any unwholesome talk come out of
your mouths, but only what is helpful for building
others up according to their needs, that it may
benefit those who listen.

Ephesians 4:29, NIV

It was grade twelve. I had a job as a telemarketer for a steam-cleaning company, and I was on top of the world.

"Hi, this is Darlene from Success Carpet Cleaning. I'm calling to let you know about our half-price carpet-cleaning offer. That's where we'll clean your living room, dining room and hall, for only $39.95..."

The secret was to get as much of our spiel out without interruption, finally closing with, "We have an opening on Monday afternoon, can we get you in then?"

My friend Lisi and I were two of their best employees. She was a blue-haired punk rocker, with the tallest Mohawk in town, and I was preppy in pink. We were opposite in so many ways, but one thing we both had in common is that we knew how to sell.

It was stressful at times, but even so, I loved the nights I spent in that office. I liked the friends that I made, and most of all, I liked the fact that the office was about 100 feet from the front door of my house.

I was juggling six shifts a week, along with my school work, youth group, a new boyfriend, exams… when I finally realized it was all just too much.

It wasn't that I wanted to quit my job really, I just knew it was time to hang up the phone and get some studying done. And so, I sat down across from my boss, lost all composure, and started to cry.

"It's okay," she said, handing me a tissue. "I know life is busy at times, but I don't want you to quit. Listen, why don't you take off the time that you need, and come back when you're ready? Oh, and just so you know," she added, "this conversation will stay here, between us."

Walking out of her office, I felt so relieved. How nice was that? Not very.

A few days later Lisi called me up to tell me that the boss had been imitating me at work. Apparently, she told everyone

71

about our private conversation, ugly cry and all. And I wondered, isn't anything sacred anymore? Doesn't anyone care?

Don't Go Throwing Shade

Looking back at it now, I know it was silly. She was young, inexperienced, and like anyone else, she made mistakes. But, here's the thing about mistakes: we need to grow from them. We need to step up and protect the ones we love. Likewise, if we're more concerned about tickling someone's ear than we are about our husbands, then we have some growing up to do.

WISELY DISCERN WHAT YOU HEAR AND WHAT YOU SAY, TO ENSURE IT'S IN LINE WITH GOD'S WILL.

I'm a girl. I know how much we love to talk. I also know that conversations can be helpful when they bring healing to a situation. What's not so helpful is when we talk behind our husband's backs, throw shade, or paint him in a bad light.

Wisely Discern and Ask God for Wisdom

Some days I'm frustrated with my husband, but even so, I have a choice. I can either run and tell others about Michael's bad habits, or I can protect his reputation by keeping the details of his life where they belong—between Michael and I. And so, I need to pray for wisdom in this area, to ensure that I'm both respecting and protecting his reputation. A good rule of thumb is to ask yourself, whether this conversation will weaken or benefit your marriage.

Seeking the counsel of a friend from a place of compassion with a desire to heal is different than sitting around the table gossiping about our husband's faults with other wives, or slandering our husbands because of the pain we've endured.

This is important to remember when it comes to the big trials we face, but it's also important to practice the same level of compassion when it comes to the trivial things that get under our skin.

The thing about confiding in your friends is that they're only getting one side of the story. And what are they giving you back? Advice that could possibly damage your marriage, if they're not a wise and trusted source. So, be careful when you're treading on these waters, as an underlying current could quickly pull you down.

Take everything to prayer. Wisely discern what you hear and what you say, to ensure it's in line with God's will and for the benefit of your marriage.

Today's Marriage Vow
To Protect Your Reputation

Today's Challenge
Whether you're talking to your friends, your family, or your children, protect your husband's reputation by being careful with the words that you choose.

Appreciate the Little Things

_____

_____

_____

_____

_____

_____

_____

_____

_____

_____

Dear Heavenly Father,

Some days I'm frustrated with my husband, but even so I always have a choice. I can run to my friends and complain about everything he's done and said, or I can bite my tongue and extend him some grace.

Whether I'm seeking the counsel of wise friend, or sitting down for a chat with a group of women, remind me to wisely discern what I hear and what I say, to ensure it's in line with Your will.

Help me to practice compassion when it comes to the trivial things that get under my skin. Give me the strength to let go where I must, and the wisdom to pray when I should.

In the name of Jesus, I pray. Amen.

DAY
10

To Love You

But God demonstrates his own love for us in this:
While we were still sinners, Christ died for us.
Romans 5:8, NIV

Imagine you go out on a Saturday afternoon and buy the car of your dreams—the one you've been saving your entire life for. After driving this beautiful car off the lot, you see one, then another, and another... Soon you realize that every single car on the road is identical to yours, in fact, they're free to anyone who walks through the door.

With that, the excitement you had is gone. Why? Because man has a natural desire to be recognized for who he is, and loved for what he's accomplished. But to the wretched man who can't afford a car? To him this gift is everything.

66 ————————————————

LOGIC TELLS US THAT LOVE IS EARNED. GOD HAS SHOWN US THAT LOVE IS A GIFT.

———————————————— 99

Logic Tells Us It's Earned

We work hard—we achieve. We study—we get good grades. We're good looking—we get dates. We exercise—we're in shape. We're friendly—we have friends. We have money—we can buy. We're loving—we're loved back.

Logic tells us that love is earned. God has shown us that love is a gift.

In the parable of the prodigal son we read about a young man who asked his father for his share of the estate. He traveled off to a far land where he squandered his inheritance. Long story short, he left full and returned empty.

With nothing to offer his Father but the rags on his back, he made his way home. And what did the Father do when he saw him coming down the road?

"But while he was still a long way off, his father saw him and was filled with compassion for him; he ran to his son, threw his arms around him and kissed him.

The son said to him, 'Father, I have sinned against heaven and against you. I am no longer worthy to be called your son.'

But the father said to his servants, 'Quick! Bring the best robe and put it on him. Put a ring on his finger and sandals on his feet. Bring the fattened calf and kill it. Let's have a feast and celebrate. For this son of mine was dead and is alive again; he was lost and is found.' So, they began to celebrate." (Luke 15:20-24, NIV)

Naturally the older brother was angry. This didn't make sense. He stood by his father working all of those years, while his brother was gone. He earned his father's respect. Didn't he also earn love?

Love Doesn't Make Sense

The thing is, love doesn't make sense. It's foolishness to this world. It goes against our desire to be recognized for what we have done and loved for who we have been. But to the sinner who understands the depth of his sin, it's everything.

This kind of love—agape love—reflects the unconditional love of our Lord. He loved us before we loved Him.

Love goes against our natural desire to seek our own well-being before that of another.

We come out of the womb screaming. We want to be loved, we want to be held, we want to be fed, and we want to be seen. But as we grow we learn how to love, hold, see, and feed others. We learn how it's more important to give than it is to receive. We learn that patience and kindness don't always come easy. And we learn that putting aside our pride is one of the hardest things we'll ever do in this life. And why do we do it? Because He loved us.

An Outward Expression of Faith

Love is an outward expression of faith. And, as we grow in love, we must begin the work of a crucifixion within us. A putting aside of envy and pride. The destruction of arrogance, envy, and greed. We must be willing to destroy this body of sin that keeps from loving as Jesus loved us.

A good wife is a loving wife. If my house is perfectly clean but I don't have love, my home is empty.

A good mother is a loving mother. If I go to every soccer practice, concert, and bake sale, but I don't love the way that God has taught me to love, my work is in vain.

And if I give up my life for the church, teaching Sunday School, hosting Bible Studies, and paying tithes, but I don't have love, I am nothing but a clanging cymbal making her noise in this world.

Today's Marriage Vow
To Love You

Today's Challenge
Find a special, out of the ordinary kind of way to tell your
husband you love him. Write him a note?
Send him a text? Make him a card?

Appreciate the Little Things

_____

_____

_____

_____

_____

_____

_____

_____

_____

_____

Dear Heavenly Father,

Looking to the Bible, I see the story of the prodigal son. I see a father who loved his son regardless of where he had been or what he had done.

I see Ruth who gave up everything she held dear to follow her mother-in-law Naomi into an unfamiliar land.

I read about Jacob who served seven years for Rachel. "They seemed unto him but a few days, for the love he had to her" (Genesis 29:20). And then he served another seven.

I read about Elkanah who was a great comfort to his wife Hannah in her time of sorrow. (1 Samuel 1)

I see a love greater yet, when we look to Your Son who gave up His life on the cross.

Thank you for showing me the depth of true love. Help me to model that kind of love in my marriage.

In the name of Jesus, I pray. Amen.

DAY
11

To Listen in the Best Way
I Know How

My dear brothers and sisters, take note of this:
Everyone should be quick to listen, slow to speak
and slow to become angry.

James 1:19, NIV

Poetry... I've read Dr. Seuss. Does that count?

Ask me to write a poem, and I'm lost. Seriously. I wouldn't know a good poem if it was staring me in the face. On the other hand, my niece Stephanie is an incredible poet. At least I *think* she is. I've never known enough about poems to tell for sure, but she puts pen to paper and off she goes, creating beautiful words. The fact that she does it with ease tells me she knows what she's doing.

Several years ago, she told me they were having an "open mic night" at a bookstore downtown, and asked me to come along.

Why not? I figured it would be a fun way to spend an evening with her. The only problem is that it wasn't exactly fun. It was kind of boring to be honest with you. Every writer had about 10 minutes to read while the rest of us spent the time picking at hang nails, surveying the crowd, and counting the number of chairs in the room—anything to keep us from falling asleep.

The only people who seemed to be enjoying themselves were the ones standing up on the stage. One-by-one they took their place up at the mic, excited to share their words with the world. Once their ten minutes of fame had ended, they had a few of their own hangnails to pull.

Later that week, I asked Stephanie why she hadn't stepped up with the rest of the writers. Why didn't she read her poems?

Her answer is one that stuck with me for years. She said that she used to be a big part of that crowd, but what she realized after a while wasn't that they came to listen, but that they came to be heard. She made a choice back then that she wanted to give herself to the art instead of taking something away. Sounds like a true poet to me.

It's true to life too, isn't it? While most of us want to be heard, we're not as eager to listen.

66

ANGER WILL NEVER GET US AS FAR AS PATIENCE AND UNDERSTANDING WILL.

99

It's More Than Lending an Ear

It's more than lending an ear, it's taking the time to consider the words of another.

It's the difference between greeting someone at your front door and inviting them into your home. When we entertain a person, we welcome them in, we show them respect, and we pay attention to them.

And, so it is with ideas and words. When we truly listen to someone, we welcome their words, respect what they say, and pay attention to them.

The quicker we listen, the less likely we are to be angry, and the more likely we are to make peace. Anger will never get us as far as patience and understanding will, and so we must practice showing our love, holding our tongues, and wisely choosing our words.

Back in the early years of our marriage, I didn't understand what Michael needed from me. My idea of listening to him was searching for a solution before it was my turn to speak.

Some days he'd tell me about a bad day at work. and by the end of the conversation we were both more frustrated than we were at the start.

It wasn't until he finally said, "I just need you to listen. That's all. I'm not looking for a magic solution—I just need a compassionate ear."

And so, listening has become a part of my vow. My goal is to listen to him and to consider his words before I speak an encouraging word.

Listening gives you an opportunity to connect with your spouse in ways you might otherwise miss, but it has to start with a caring heart. Thoughtful enough to put distractions aside. Considerate enough to lean in and listen. Selfless enough to try and see things his way.

Today's Marriage Vow
To Listen in the Best Way I Know How

Today's Challenge
Practice listening from a place of compassion and grace. Let go of distractions, and try to see things his way.

Appreciate the Little Things

_____

_____

_____

_____

_____

_____

_____

_____

_____

_____

Dear Heavenly Father,

Teach me the importance of laying down my pride, so that I might communicate well.

Remind me to listen far more than I speak. Taking the time to consider his words that I might understand him more than I do.

Help me to choose my words wisely, and to be an encouraging wife.

Thank You for listening to me in the amazing way that You do. Thank You for hearing and receiving my words.

In the name of Jesus, I pray. Amen.

DAY
12

To Walk Through This Life with You

Two are better than one, because they have a good return for their labor: if either of them falls down, one can help the other up. But pity anyone who falls and has no one to help them up.

Ecclesiastes 4:9-10, NIV

I had just stepped into the hallway when I happened upon the most beautiful thing one could see—the undying love between a man and his wife. Holding each other close, I knew they were every bit as in love as they had been some 60 years before, when they said their "I do's."

Dad was smiling, and Mom was whispering what I could only imagine were encouraging words as she gently brushed his cheek with her hand. A warm reminder that she was the bride of his youth and he was her groom.

The Mark of a Great Couple

What is the mark of a great couple? What makes you stop and say to yourself, "They're still in love after all of these years?"

If you're anything like me, you notice the signs. They're often subtle, but nevertheless they're consistent. They cherish each other, they have a deep respect for each other, and they honour the sacred vows they once made.

Some couples simply grow old, while others grow old *together*. They respect their relationship enough to *work* it out instead of *stepping* out.

Couples like this aren't perfect. In fact, I'd venture to guess that most of them have done and said things that hurt. And, just like us, they're human beings walking in grace.

We're constantly faced with challenges that threaten to tear our marriage apart. Disrespect, pride, financial stress, sickness, unemployment, disappointment, and a lack of communication are a few things among many that have the potential to weaken our bond, and so we must strengthen that bond by being humble and gentle and kind.

Be completely humble and gentle; be patient, bearing with one another in love. Make every effort to keep the unity of the Spirit through the bond of peace. (Ephesians 4:2-3, NIV)

Strength in Numbers

Every marriage goes through seasons of hardship, and each one of those seasons give us an opportunity to strengthen our bond and increase our faith. But here's the thing about staying the course, we need to keep fighting *together*. Why? Because, there's strength in numbers. In fact, the Bible tells us that a strand of three cords is not quickly broken.

A STRAND OF THREE CORDS IS NOT QUICKLY BROKEN.

Michael and I are like two sides of a coin. We're opposite in so many ways, and yet I need that contrast in my life to balance me out. In most cases, I'm impatient while he's overly cautious. I am a fly-by-the-seat-of-my-pants kind of girl, while Michael is a plan-every-detail-for-years kind of guy. Together we're good. I remind him to step out in faith, while he reminds me to count the cost before jumping too quick.

Our children get the best of both worlds. One parent is the strong silent type, while the other is a nurturing compassionate type. We're stronger together, because we draw from each other's strengths.

He lifts me up when I'm down, which is possibly what I love the most about him. Likewise, he leans on my strength. Sometimes I wonder how. How can I possibly be a source of strength to this man? I'm not strong. I'm a girl who ugly-cries at a wedding. But the thing is, I'm ready to listen, share in his burden, and I'm able to pray. And, when we do pray? We're adding a third cord to our strand.

It's a Life That Gives Back

It's a beautiful thing when a husband and wife are willing to sacrifice for the good of their marriage and are dedicated to making it work. It's a life-long commitment of giving, and serving, and yielding ourselves to God's will, but it's also a life that gives back in so many ways. Love, respect, honor, and friendship are just a few of the blessings that come with sowing compassion and care.

It's more than simply living together: It's experiencing life together; It's facing hardships together; It's building a family together; It's growing together.

Today's Marriage Vow
To Walk Through This Life with You

Today's Challenge
If your husband is sick, troubled or weary be a
companion that remains by his side.

Appreciate the Little Things

_____

_____

_____

_____

_____

_____

_____

_____

_____

Dear Heavenly Father,

Sometimes we go down difficult paths, but overall it is a beautiful journey. We started out as friends and we're building this friendship year after year.

The stress of everyday life can be taxing, and the weight of the world can tear us apart if we let it. Keep us together, Lord, whatever may come.

Teach me the importance of making sacrifices for the sake of my marriage. Help me to prioritize my relationship, and to make time for my husband.

Your Word tells us that a friend must show himself friendly, and so I'm asking that You help me to be pleasant and kind, gracious and loving.

Teach me to learn and to grow from disagreements. I have an opportunity to open my mind to what my husband is feeling and thinking. Give me the wisdom to process these thoughts and to handle them wisely.

In the name of Jesus, I pray. Amen.

DAY
13

To Be a Woman of Strength

She is clothed with strength and dignity;
she can laugh at the days to come.
Proverbs 31:25, NIV

As the weather warms up and the flowers wake up from their slumber, I'm reminded of bonfires, barbecues, beaches, and bowls of fresh fruit. I'm reminded of an amusement park not far from here that's on our to-do list each year.

I love the ebb and flow of the classic melody. Children laughing, music playing, gears moving, and of course the rumbling sound of the roller coaster.

Life's Up and Downs

As I got to thinking about that today, I was reminded how life is like that roller coaster some days–we have our ups and we our downs. But even when we think that life isn't going the way that we hoped it would be, we can rest assured knowing that God will lift us back up.

THE GIANTS WE CONQUER ARE AS BREAD TO OUR SOUL.

When the Bible talks about the woman in Proverbs 31, it tells us that she laughs without fear of the future. I see a woman who is confident in the Lord she serves, and His ability to care for her needs. I see a woman who's even-keeled through the ups and the downs, knowing that obstacles offer her an opportunity to grow stronger in faith. I see a woman who has placed her future in His capable hands. Hands that are able to mold and to shape us. Hands that are wisely directing our steps.

The Bible tells us that the eyes of the Lord search the earth, to strengthen those who are committed to him. And, so we see that our strength doesn't come from ourselves, it comes from the Lord.

Caleb, a Man of Courage and Strength

You don't hear all that much about Caleb, but you should if you're looking for an example of courage and strength. You hear about Moses leading the children of Israel out of Egypt. You hear about Joshua crossing the Jordan and fighting at the battle of Jericho, but few lines are given to Caleb, a man of incredible faith. I'll tell you, the more I'm reading about him, the more I'm intrigued by his courage and strength.

The word Caleb means "dog," and rightly so, as he ferociously protected the children of God. I imagine a "Dog the Bounty Hunter" kind of guy with a hard shell and a soft heart. Someone who was willing to step up and get the job done.

He wasn't merely a faithful companion to Joshua, he was faithful to God in all of his ways. Our husbands need that kind of strength in their lives—someone who is willing to fiercely protect their marriage and stand by their side whatever may come. Someone who's willing to rise to the occasion when he needs support.

You might remember the story in Numbers chapter 13 where Moses sent out 12 men to spy on Canaan. While 10 were afraid to go back to the land of the giants, Caleb was right there with Joshua, ready and willing to take them all on.

"Only rebel not ye against the Lord, neither fear ye the people of the land; for they are bread for us: their defence

is departed from them, and the Lord is with us: fear them not." (KJV)

Bread to Our Soul

"They are bread for us," he said. You see, Caleb saw what many Christians fail to see—that trials are the very thing that strengthen us. The giants we conquer are as bread to our soul, and by the power of God working in us and through us, we grow.

Too many give up when the going gets tough. Financial strain, a distant spouse, lack of romance, lust, boredom, loneliness, and pride are just a few of the giants we face.

I don't think it's a coincidence that we read about giants in scripture. Their presence and their demise are reminders that God is mighty to save.

The Israelites were fearful, but Caleb and Joshua followed the Lord regardless of those things they had seen. They recognized the source of their strength, and knew that power within them was greater than that from without.

Likewise, marriage is a journey of sorts. Some days it's flowing with milk and honey, and other days we're facing a giant or two. On the days that you're weary, fearful, and down, will you give up like the ten who turned back? Or are willing to fight by the power of God working in you and through you to complete His good work.

Today's Marriage Vow
To Be a Woman of Strength

Today's Challenge
Seek to bless your husband by letting him know you'll do your best to rise to the challenges that come your way.

Appreciate the Little Things

_____

_____

_____

_____

_____

_____

_____

_____

_____

_____

Dear Heavenly Father,

Give me peace in the midst of my trials.

Remind me to rejoice on the darkest of days knowing that the trying of my faith builds patience.

Teach me to lean on You and to put my trust in You at all times. For You have never failed me in the past and will never fail me in the future.

Give me the strength to face each day with laughter, knowing that all things work out together for good to those who are in Christ Jesus.

In the name of Jesus, I pray. Amen.

To Guard the Castle from Harm

She watches over the affairs of her household
and does not eat the bread of idleness.

Proverbs 31:27, NIV

It was Friday night.

After 30 years I still remember that, because we had gone over to my sister's house for a Bible study like we did every Friday. About 15 of us would get together in their basement to sing, pray, and search scripture together.

It had been a long day and our son Brendan (a baby at the time) was more than ready to grab some sleep. We all were. Turning into the driveway, I was relieved to finally be home.

Suddenly Michael stopped the car short. He fell silent before putting it back in reverse. Cranking my head to look past the fence, I notice the back door was wide open. For all that we knew someone could be inside. It was safer for us to pull into a friend's driveway, and call the police from their phone. Thankfully Michael was leading the way.

An hour later, the officers walked us into our little house to survey the damage and take down our statements. How long were we gone? What did they take? What did they do?

They didn't take much, since we didn't have all that much at the time other than a few CDs, a stereo system and a little VCR called a movie machine. What they did take, however was our sense of peace. They violated our home, and our trust.

It took weeks—maybe months until I felt safe again. I knew that they weren't watching me through the windows, but I couldn't shake that feeling of being vulnerable and exposed. It was time to step up security to keep our home safe.

Protect the Sanctity of Your Family

My vow today is to guard the castle from harm. When I'm talking about the castle however, I'm not talking about the little house on the corner, the laptops, or a flat screen TV. Those are material things that one can replace. What I am talking about here is the role of a watchman who protects the sanctity of the family.

In Ezekiel chapter 3 we see that God had appointed Ezekiel as a watchman. In those days, towers were built so that a watchman could stand guard to look over the fields or the gates of a city. Because of its height, one could see the enemy approaching from a distance, giving them enough time to sound a warning. He saw who went in, and he saw who went out. Becoming familiar with the people therein, he witnessed the beauty of everyday life as it unfolded before him.

The Bible instructs older women to teach the younger women to be good keepers of their home. It's common sense to keep a house clean, isn't it? But wiser yet is a woman who keeps a close watch over her home.

66

IF WE DON'T TAKE HOLD OF TEMPTATION, TEMPTATION WILL TAKE HOLD OF US.

99

In Titus 2:5 we find the words, "keepers at home." Looking to the Strong's Concordance we see it does indeed refer to the domestic role of taking care of household affairs, but it also includes this meaning: "the (watch or) keeper of the house." Coming from the root word "ouros" meaning "a guard."

When we're involved with our children we get to know the people in their lives. We see who's coming, who's going, and who's talking to who. We know what to pray for, because we're close knit.

Guard Your Marriage

Guard your marriage by protecting your heart from the enemy. Resist temptation when it knocks at your door. Take your mind captive by casting down any negative thoughts, should they try to creep in. Doubts that tempt you to give up on your marriage. Temptations that take your eyes off of your husband. Pride that stands in the way of doing what's right. Thoughts that lead to resentment.

The Bible tells us that the devil is lurking around, like a lion that's stalking its prey. He's cunning and sly, which is why we need to be wise and alert.

When we toy with these doubts and desires, we're playing with fire. We're putting ourselves right where the enemy wants us—at the end of his hook. And, if we don't take hold of temptation, temptation will take hold of us.

Remember the story of David and Bathsheba? He didn't go looking for temptation, temptation found him, which goes to show us that we can be tempted anywhere and at any time.

Prepare yourself by taking thoughts captive, resisting temptation, and guarding your heart.

Today's Marriage Vow
To Guard the Castle from Harm

Today's Challenge
Protect the sanctity of your marriage by keeping
watch over your home.

Appreciate the Little Things

Dear Heavenly Father,

Thank you for keeping us safe in Your hands, and close to Your heart.

I'm thankful for your Word which reminds me how important it is to stand guard of my home, to watch over my marriage, and to protect my heart from the enemy. I can't do this alone, Lord. I need Your help. I need Your power and grace. I need Your strength. I need You to lead me in wisdom to safety.

Help me to be a watchman who fiercely protects her marriage, and help me to guard it from harm.

In the name of Jesus, I pray. Amen.

DAY

15

To Give You My Best

A wife of noble character is her husband's crown,
but a disgraceful wife is like decay in his bones.
Proverbs 12:4, NIV

About ten years ago I was interviewed by the local newspaper. I assumed it was because I had just co-authored *Reshaping it All* with Candace Cameron Bure. It was a New York Times best-seller, which at the time was all the buzz in our house.

The next day when the paper came out, I was featured in an article titled, "Joyfully Serving Your Husband." It practically filled the page, with a headline so bold it couldn't be missed.

That didn't go over so well in our city. In fact, there were plenty of people willing to voice their opinion in opposition of serving. Not only that—they didn't like the fact that I'd dress up for my husband, that I would have dinner ready on the stove when he got home from work, or that I would touch up my makeup before he got home. They were appalled that I'd even suggest such a thing in this day and age.

The article caused such an uproar that I was featured three times in the paper that week.

The following excerpt, written by Tom Oleson, wisely put things in perspective:

MAYBE YOU STOPPED CARING AS MUCH AS YOU USED TO.

This seems so quaint that it will be almost comical to liberated women—and their male fellow travellers—at least those who are not absolutely enraged by it, all those years of frustrated feminism only to be finally advised to look feminine during "his" dinner?

On the same page as the article about Schacht is an article advising the modern woman how to cope with getting her image online. The advice is pretty simple and direct. In fact, it's a lot like Schacht's advice, except there's nothing about dinner, perhaps because cooking is about the only thing you can't do online these days. The modern woman is advised to spruce up her image so she looks good on screen, perhaps get a new and flattering picture taken so she will look even better on screen and pose herself attractively to make a good impression.

That's probably all sound advice, but which woman is truly the ridiculous figure here—the woman who makes herself attractive for the husband she knows; or the woman who makes herself attractive to people she doesn't know, people whom she has to impress "within the first few seconds?" Maybe a world in which Schacht seems out of place but our hi-tech Modern Ms. fits right in needs to check its priorities, to try a little reality check.

How many of us are doing this? Are we more concerned about impressing the world than our husbands?

When we're with other people we give them our best. We're happy, we're positive, we're encouraging, and we're fun. But what happens when we close the front door? Are we just as fun and exciting? Are we just as respectful?

You May Have Changed Over Time

You often hear couples say that the other has changed. Maybe you have? Maybe you stopped caring as much as you used to. Maybe you stopped putting him first like you used to.

If you want your marriage to flourish, put in the effort it takes to give him your best.

When Michael and I were dating, we spent every hour we could together. We watched movies, went for long walks, had picnics in the park, and hung out at the mall. We made time for each other by putting our relationship first.

I know there are various seasons in life, and some of those seasons, can drain us of energy and take up our time. But, it doesn't take much to show him you care. Michael and I go for a drive every morning. It's not much. We just pick up a coffee at a drive through, and then we come home, but the thing is we're spending the first part of our day doing something together.

Our Treasure Dictates Our Actions

Our actions will always depend on the things that we treasure the most, and so, the more that we treasure our husbands the more our actions will follow.

How do we treasure our husbands? By learning to love them, and yes, love *can* be learned. We learn it from watching our Savior and following His example of love. We learn it from reading, and being transformed by God's Word. We learn it from the Holy Spirit Who guides us, convicts us, and teaches us to walk in God's truth.

Today's Marriage Vow
To Give You My Best

Today's Challenge
Put in the effort it takes to give him your best.

Appreciate the Little Things

_____

_____

_____

_____

_____

_____

_____

_____

_____

_____

Dear Heavenly Father,

I don't want to settle for half-measures. I want a marriage that's filled with friendship, respect, and intimacy. Help us to rekindle our love for one another, and to keep the passion between us alive.

I know that a strong marriage doesn't just happen, it's built by two people who passionately pursue a strong bond.

Remind me to be thoughtful and gentle with my husband's heart. Give me a hunger for intimacy and a desire for nobody else but him. May all I do and say come from a place of kindness, governed by peace, and perfected by the bond of love.

Show me the best ways to be affectionate. Remind me to consider him first, to always be warm and compassionate, and to give him my best.

In the name of Jesus, I pray. Amen.

DAY
16

To Love You Without Expectations

Sow your seed in the morning, and at evening let your
hands not be idle, for you do not know which will
succeed, whether this or that, or whether both
will do equally well.
Ecclesiastes 11:6, NIV

It was a beautiful May afternoon, when suddenly an idea popped into my head. I wanted to buy the two-story house on the corner with the cedar shingles and the old-fashioned front porch. With three bedrooms, it was the perfect sized house for our growing family, not to mention the fact that I loved the raspberry bushes and grape vines that lined the back fence.

It had just come up on the market, and I couldn't wait to tell Michael. At the same time, I wondered if he'd even consider saying goodbye to our sweet little home, and increasing our mortgage again.

I spent the afternoon dreaming about the garden I'd plant, what we'd do with the barn style shed, and all of the blankets I'd pin on that clothesline. I dreamed about raspberry muffins, and homemade grape jelly. I imagined myself spending warm summer nights on the front porch of that house.

Without further ado, I designed a plan. I would pray. In fact, I would pray so hard that God would be sure to hear every word that I said.

And so, I went home, got down on my knees and prayed the most earnest prayer I could muster.

Sometimes Expectations Fall Short

I had one request, and no, I wasn't asking God for a house—I asked Him for peace. That was my only request. I wanted to discuss this idea with Michael, but above anything else, I didn't want this house to come between us. I didn't want Michael to feel as though I was boxing him in or adding financial stress to our marriage. All I wanted was unity and peace.

After dinner we settled down for a nice quiet talk, which was anything but unified or peaceful. Word after word spiralled out of control, and before I knew it we were each sitting in our own corner of the house wondering how things escalated so quickly. Where was the harmony and peace I had prayed for? Why was this happening?

That night, after Michael and the kids went to bed I sat on the couch weeping and praying again. I can't tell you how disappointed I was. The one thing I wanted more than anything else was to just get along. The house didn't matter to me anymore; I was just so upset that things had turned ugly and tense.

> ## A FLOWER DOESN'T BLOOM BECAUSE WE WANT IT TO, IT BLOOMS IN ITS OWN TIME ACCORDING TO THE WILL OF GOD.

I had tried to be kind and considerate. With everything in me I tried to avoid fighting with him. At the end of the day, my expectations fell short, and we were both left hurting over a stupid thing like a house.

Where was God in all this? Didn't He hear the words I so earnestly prayed? Didn't He know that I just wanted peace?

His Wisdom is Greater Than Mine

The next morning Michael got out of bed with full intentions of buying that house. Something had changed him that morning. Something brought peace to his soul and unified us in a way that only God can.

I've learned a big lesson when it comes to the Lord: His wisdom is far greater than mine. When we truly believe that He takes care of our needs, that He establishes our steps, and that He is powerful enough to change our situation at any given time, we can rest in His wisdom and strength.

Nothing is perfect. Plans fall apart. People come, others go. We live in a fallen world in which we're often let down, but while we look for the good, God gives us the best.

We Can't Control the Choices They Make

Remember, a flower doesn't bloom because we want it to, it blooms in its own time according to the will of God. Our husbands are no different—we can't control the choices they make. All we can do is love them in the best way we know how.

Our job is go about planting seeds of encouragement, patience, kindness, and love. What God does with those seeds is His business, not ours.

We need be mindful of each other—more mindful in fact, than we are of ourselves. Ready to let go of expectations that separate and divide. Tender-hearted in the face of disappointment. Patient while we're waiting on God.

Today's Marriage Vow
To Love You Without Expectation

Today's Challenge
Do your part to plant seeds, but patiently leave
the heart work to God.

Appreciate the Little Things

_____

_____

_____

_____

_____

_____

_____

_____

_____

Dear Heavenly Father,

Help me to be patient with my husband, and to offer him grace. To remember that we all make mistakes. To be tender-hearted, ready and willing to forgive him in the face of disappointment.

Help me to be mindful of him—more mindful in fact, than I am of myself. Ready to let go of expectations that separate and divide. Help me to let go of my need to have things my own way.

Remind me to stay positive and to look for the good in him. Give me the strength to exercise contentment in all situations.

Give me the wisdom to communicate well as we clarify our needs and our wants.

And finally, thank You for the grace that You give me time after time.

In the name of Jesus, I pray. Amen.

DAY
17

To Celebrate Our Differences

For just as each of us has one body with many members,
and these members do not all have the same function,
so in Christ we, though many, form one body, and
each member belongs to all the others.

Romans 12:4-5, NIV

I don't particularly love shopping with Michael. I enjoy doing a lot of things with him, but walking around a mall together is not at the top of either one of our lists.

Not that I don't like going to the mall—or walking with my husband—it's just that when it comes to being shopping buddies we're not the best fit.

I'd much rather shop with my daughter who doesn't mind hemming and hawing for 20 minutes over a pair of shoes and then coming back to them again and again. We're both the same way, shopping is like hunting to us. The thrill of the pursuit is every bit as exciting as the final catch. Walking from store to store, we continue to hunt until our ankles give out.

> **CELEBRATE THE CONTRAST YOU FIND IN YOUR MARRIAGE, AS YOU VIEW IT THROUGH THE LENS OF GOD'S GRACE.**

Michael's idea of shopping is walking into a store, picking up the same brand of jeans, paying for them, and heading back to the car. There's no browsing, there's no looking around, there's no wasting time at the mall. He's in and he's out faster than I can say, "Should we buy this?"

Then there's the home furnishing store, where we find the inspiration we've been looking for to decorate our homes. Starting on the right-hand side of the store, my daughter and I make our way down every isle, carefully checking for any new deals, any dent or scratch sales, and any out of the ordinary decor that catches our eye. The budget is tight, so it's imperative that we find the best bargain we can possibly find.

I picked up an incredible spice rack a while back that looks like a vintage piece. It hangs on the wall in our kitchen near the payphone and, since it's fairly large, it fits all of my spices. I've also found some vintage-style mailboxes that add a touch of cuteness to my office wall.

Michael doesn't get my way of shopping. He wouldn't spend six hours at the mall, nor would he spend six dollars on an item just because it's cute. He doesn't get excited about wicker baskets or toss cushions the way I do. But then again, I don't get excited about canoes and hiking the way he does.

We're Two Very Different People

Like most of my friends, I enjoy the little touches that make our house a home. He has a box of tools that make our house a home. We're two different people with two very different mindsets. I like pretty and he likes practical. I love having a few extra cushions on the couch, a bouquet of flowers on the table, and quilted blankets on the bed. Michael likes sitting on the couch, sound equipment on the table, and a weighted blanket on the bed.

If I continued to list the many ways we are different, my words would be endless. We're like two pieces of one puzzle: so different, yet, we're designed to fit together as one.

The Key to Acceptance

For the most part, our differences work in our favor. But like anyone else, we have days when they don't. Days when we're frustrated because we just don't agree. Days when we're so different the puzzle pieces don't fit.

Dave Meurer writes, "A great marriage is not when the 'perfect couple' come together. It is when an imperfect couple learns to enjoy their differences."

The key to acceptance is grace. We're all a work in progress, aren't we? The word progress goes hand in hand with growth, not perfection. It's an onward motion to the goal ahead. It's recognizing the fact that we're every bit as imperfect as our husbands. It's allowing them room to grow into the people they are, not the men we expect them to be. It's learning to appreciate our differences, by celebrating the men they have become.

What would life be without contrast? Without night and day? Without black and white? Without mountains and valleys? Without sweet and sour? Without treble and bass? It would all be rather dull, wouldn't it?

Celebrate the contrast you find in your marriage, as you view it through the lens of God's glorious grace.

Today's Marriage Vow
To Celebrate Our Differences

Today's Challenge
Look for contrast in your marriage, and celebrate the
differences you find.

Appreciate the Little Things

_____

_____

_____

_____

_____

_____

_____

_____

_____

_____

Dear Heavenly Father,

Like a piece of art, uniquely created, we're formed by Your hands. No two people are alike. No two have the same character. No two possess the same qualities. We have differing roles in this marriage—unique gifts blending together to bring forth Your glory. Teach us to embrace our differences, to accept who we are, and to use our gifts to grow stronger together.

Help me to see the beauty in being unique and to accept my husband for who he is. We have different ideas, we have our own passions, and we have opinions that don't always match. Help me to open my heart as I'm learning to understand him.

Give me patience and kindness when we don't see eye to eye. Remind me to slow down and consider his thoughts before I insist on my own. It can take a lifetime for us to truly understand each other, which is why we need Your wisdom and strength working through us.

In the name of Jesus, I pray. Amen.

DAY
18

To Work as a Unified Team

That all of them may be one, Father, just as you are in me and
I am in you. May they also be in us so that the world may
believe that you have sent me.

John 17:21, NIV

Our family loves to play games at the table: "Trivial Pursuit" to
be exact. Since the kids were young, we've always played in
teams, as I find that teams even the playing field. We eat, we
play, and we laugh until we cry.

As I got to thinking about that today, I realized that some
of the greatest lessons in love are learned at that table. We're
patient and kind when we're working together, we're not

jealous or envious when our partner scores a point, or angry when they get one wrong. It's our opponent we're not kind-hearted with—in a playful way of course. But for those on our team, we encourage, we cheer, and we rejoice with each other. Together we strive for the prize.

Imagine how much love would grow if we all realized that we're on the same team. If we stopped to think for a minute who the real enemy was, and started fighting against him together. An enemy that seeks to destroy marriages, tear friendships apart, dismantle churches, and disrupt unity in the home. If we put down our pride and picked up our cross. If we stopped quarrelling with one other and chose instead to strive for the prize. If we put aside all jealousy and spurred each other on. If we traded our anger for grace. Not just when it's easy, but on the most difficult days.

A team is more than a group or a couple. It's members working together toward common goals. In the same way, a husband and wife can either be a couple or they can be a couple that's also a team. The question is, are you working together toward common goals, or merely living under the same roof?

In John chapter 17 we read how Jesus prayed in the Garden of Gethsemane just hours before his death. As we read through the chapter, you can't help but see that unity was heavy upon His heart. In fact, in that one chapter alone, He appealed to the Father five times on our behalf asking for unity among believers.

Unity Bears Witness to God

If you've ever wondered why unity is so important to Jesus, we find the answer in verse 21.

That all of them may be one, Father, just as you are in me and I am in you. May they also be in us so that the world may believe that you have sent me. (John 17:21, NIV)

God calls us to be a unified church, and so, let's start with a unified marriage. When a couple is unified they bear witness to God. When people see love, they see Christ.

We're called to bear witness of Him, not merely with words, but with actions that bring us to the cross time and again. Love that bring us down to our knees in prayer petitioning on behalf of our marriage.

66

GOD CALLS US TO BE A UNIFIED CHURCH, AND SO, LET'S START WITH A UNIFIED MARRIAGE.

99

In order to build a healthy relationship, we need to be working together as one, with all of the strength that we have. A team, where each one esteems the other higher than themselves, and where each one is willing to give more than they take.

Love Isn't Fair

One of the most difficult things we've had to learn over time is how to work as a team. I remember the days when my kids had to learn this in school. Every year without fail, the teacher assigned a group project. And every year they complained that it just wasn't fair. Somebody on the team wasn't trying. Someone wasn't doing their share of the work. Someone was getting a free ride...

And, so it is with life, sometimes teamwork isn't fair. Sometimes my husband is outside shoveling snow while I'm inside a warm house sipping tea. Sometimes he's lifting heavy furniture while I'm folding sheets. And sometimes I'm cooking a big meal while he's on the phone.

Then I'm reminded of the many times we've carried each other over the years. The days when I was down and he lifted me up, the times when he was overwhelmed and I helped him find peace.

I've come to learn that while teamwork is hard, it's worth striving for. We've seen how love gives without keeping score, and that some days it calls us to a place of grace. I know that love isn't fair, for if it was, I'd owe my Lord far more than I could possibly give.

Today's Marriage Vow
To Work as a Unified Team

Today's Challenge
Keep a candle burning throughout the day. At the same time,
continually pray for a unified marriage.

Appreciate the Little Things

_____

_____

_____

_____

_____

_____

_____

_____

_____

_____

Dear Heavenly Father,

Give me a growing hunger for more of You and Your word.

Grant me a heart of humility, so that I might be pliable clay in Your hands.

Bind us together. Unite us as one. Help us establish a mission. When we're united in faith we are stronger. When we walk by the same set of values, we sharpen each other. And, when we're focused on the truth of Your word, our marriage is built on a firm and steady foundation.

Give me the wisdom to know when and how to protect our marriage from sin. Give me the strength to stand firm when we're under attack.

In the name of Jesus, I pray. Amen.

DAY
19

To Be Gentle & Kind

A gentle answer turns away wrath, but a
harsh word stirs up anger.
Proverbs 15:1, NIV

Have you ever snapped at someone? I'm embarrassed to say that I have, about three decades ago. She was a complete stranger on the bus, and for some reason I decided that day was the day I was going to open the cage and let my ugly side out.

One could say that I was provoked, but a wiser person would say that we hold the reins to our words, and that nothing is resolved by an unconstrained tongue. In the same way that a wild horse is trained and brought to submission by a wise and gentle master, we too must learn to bridle and tame our tongue.

Whether this one said this, or that one said that, at the end of the day it's the gentle and quiet spirit that wins the most hearts.

So, what is the best way to answer someone who's rude, angry, or impolite? With the softest words we can find.

A gentle answer turns away wrath, but a harsh word stirs up anger. (Proverbs 15:1, NIV)

66 ───────────────────────────

AT THE END OF THE DAY IT'S THE GENTLE AND QUIET SPIRIT THAT WINS THE MOST HEARTS.

─────────────────────────── 99

It's like this, if someone throws a ball against a hard wall, it's going to bounce back to them. When it does they have the opportunity to throw that ball again and again. The moment they throw that ball at a soft surface, however, it absorbs the impact and the ball is no longer in play.

The Bible is telling us here to absorb the impact of anger. Just to be clear: I'm not talking about physical abuse here, I'm taking about days when your husband gets under your skin, tries your patience, or says something that makes you want to lash out in anger.

It's easy to be gentle and kind when it suits us, but true kindness gives on difficult days and extends to difficult people.

What might that look like, for you? A soft word, a smile, and a moment in prayer to soften your heart.

Our Words Have Consequences

It's hard to remember this when I'm frustrated and angry. Some days it feels like the harsh words just roll off my tongue all on their own.

But then I wonder... do they really? Is it really that hard to remember to be kind and compassionate, or could it be that during those moments when I'm tested and tried, I'm failing the test by the choices I make?

Words are like toothpaste, once the paste comes out of the tube, there's no way it's going back in. In the same way a word spoken can't be taken back. Once it's out there–it's out.

In her book *Keep it Shut*, Karen Ehman writes, "Our words are powerful, and they have consequences... Bruises fade and bones heal, but a scorched heart may take years to mend."

It might feel good in the moment to loosen your tongue, but the shockwave of repercussion can leave long-term effects. And so, the Bible instructs believers to be quick to listen and slow to speak. For in listening we soften hearts, and in speaking we minister grace.

Kindness is an Inside Job

If you're slipping into the latest fashions, and your hair looks like the cover of Vogue, but you're not gentle and kind, you have a problem that can't be concealed with cosmetics.

If we're kind on the outside and rotten on the inside, we're no different than the Pharisees who appeared religious, but inside they neglected the more important things of God like mercy and kindness and love.

This world has enough trophy wives, it has enough beauty queens, and it certainly has enough face-tuning filters. What we don't see enough are women who model faith and truth through the way that they live. We don't have enough women who treasure the unfading beauty of a gentle and quiet spirit.

Don't get me wrong, there's nothing wrong with being attractive or having a good sense of style, as long as your inner beauty is outshining it all.

Do you listen more than you speak? Do you welcome interruptions? Are you tender-hearted? Are you gentle and kind?

Don't be complacent when it comes to your marriage. Day in and day out you wake up together and you know that at the end of the day you'll be heading right back to that same room again. There's no challenge in that, but there's always a challenge in grabbing hold of and keeping his heart.

Today's Marriage Vow
To Be Gentle and Kind

Today's Challenge
Be intentional about the way you respond
to your husband. Always choose to be
gentle and kind regardless of
how you might feel.

Appreciate the Little Things

Dear Heavenly Father,

Please give me a gentle spirit, and remind me to handle my husband with care. Whether I'm having a good day, or the weight of the world is bringing me down, may I be tender and loving to him. The kind of woman who's a crown to her husband, a woman whose virtue shines bright.

May my words be gentle, my actions be kind, and my thoughts always tender and pure.

Let me be quick to hear, slow to speak, and slow to anger, looking to You as my perfect example. For You, oh Lord, are holy, just, gentle, and kind.

In the name of Jesus, I pray. Amen.

To Dream With You

I can do all this through him who
gives me strength.
Philippians 4:13, NIV

I remember them well. Those first few years I spent with my husband. The nights we walked hand in hand in the park. The days we spent dreaming of a future together, and what that future might look like.

Side-by-side, with a ruler and pencil in hand, we mapped out our house. Whether we could afford it or not wasn't the question. This was our dream home—the future we hoped to build one day with kids underfoot, and a dog the yard. We'd work hard, and someday we'd get there.

Some of the best days we had we spent dreaming. I wanted to know everything about him, including his hopes and his dreams for the future. What were his goals? Where did he want to live? How many kids did he want? Did he prefer dogs or cats? If he would have told me that he wanted to go to the moon, I would have been cheering him on every step of the way.

I was his biggest cheerleader, and he, mine. It didn't matter how big his dream was, I believed that he could and my greatest hope was to be by his side when he did.

The Power of Encouragement

Couples really never stop dreaming, but the sad thing is that too often we stop dreaming *together*. We stop communicating about the things that are important to us, the work God is calling us to, and the fears that we face.

I know that Michael is talented, he's smart, and he's a great leader, but does *he* know that? I wonder how many times a day that voice inside him tells him that he can't, he won't, and he never will.

I can't tell you the many times I've told myself I can't write. I had always wanted to be a writer, but I didn't think it was possible until one person told me I could. It goes to show that the power of encouragement goes a long way.

A greater power yet is the power of God. It's an honor to encourage my husband and to be there to remind him that when God brings you to it, He will bring you through it.

Of course, that doesn't mean that everyone who wants to go to the moon will surely land on the moon. But it does mean that when you put your trust in God He'll lead you to greater paths than you could imagine. He'll birth a great desire within you and equip you for the journey ahead.

Let God plant those desires in your heart. Let Him take the lead. And trust Him to equip you.

His dreams may be the same as yours, but sometimes they may differ. And if they are different? Handle his heart with great care. Communicate your concern with loving kindness, and bring your concerns to God asking that *His* will be done.

I BELIEVED THAT HE COULD AND MY GREATEST HOPE WAS TO BE BY HIS SIDE WHEN HE DID.

7 Ways to Dream With Your Husband

1. Start with contentment. Don't use dreaming as an excuse to lust after the world. If we aren't content with what we have today, we won't be content tomorrow. Achieving our

goals is fulfilling and it's fun, but nothing on this earth will satisfy us the way that Jesus Christ can.

2. Listen to him talk. People express their dreams all the time. Once you're aware of that, you'll start to notice.

3. Be faithfully courageous. Don't be afraid to dream big. Sarah laughed when the angel told her that she would bear a child. She was well past the age of child bearing. But God promised Abraham that he would become a great and mighty nation, and all the nations of the earth would be blessed in him. It took a leap of faith for them to accept this.

4. Be an encouragement to each other. Remember that the power of encouragement goes a long way, and our words reinforce that.

5. Spend time doing nothing. Slow down your life long enough to have heart-to-heart conversations.

6. Share your heart with him. Start talking about the future. Is there a class you hope to take? A ministry God is calling you to? Do you want a larger family? Keep the lines of communication open. Discuss your dreams and your concerns.

7. Create a mission statement for your marriage. (See Appendix I) Add your dreams to a section called "Goals and Dreams."

Today's Marriage Vow
To Dream With You

Today's Challenge
Create a mission statement for your marriage.
See Appendix I for a general guideline.

Appreciate the Little Things

_____

_____

_____

_____

_____

_____

_____

_____

_____

_____

Dear Heavenly Father,

Help us to stay together, to pray together, and to keep dreaming together because we're in this *together*—for life.

We're surrounded by negative thoughts and discouraging words. We don't need more of that. What we need more of is reassurance and encouragement that You're leading the way. Help me to be that voice of encouragement to my husband.

Teach us to communicate about the things that are important to us, the work You are calling us to, and the fears that we face.

Looking to the scriptures, we see the faithful standing back to watch as You miraculously transformed their lives. They believed in You when all hope was gone.

Give us the courage to dream together, Lord. And give us the strength to follow Your will regardless of what it might cost.

In the name of Jesus, I pray. Amen.

DAY
21

To Encourage & Edify You

Do not let any unwholesome talk come out of
your mouths, but only what is helpful for building
others up according to their needs, that it may
benefit those who listen.
Ephesians 4:29, NIV

Have you ever noticed how easy it is to find fault? It's so much
easier than pointing the finger at yourself, especially when
you're living with someone day in and day out. I notice the
dishes, I see all the spills, and every once in a while, I nag.

But then I'm reminded that love looks for the best and hopes for the best in each other, the way that my dad always looked for the best in my mom.

Dad wasn't just good at building a rec room, a deck, or a fence, he was devoted to building our family up with his words. And, so he did, with encouragement, inspiration, and hope.

The Bible tell us to comfort one another and to edify each other. What its really saying there is to build each other up with our words.

How do we do that? How do we restore and rebuild the relationships we've torn down? By comforting each other with tender-hearted encouragement, by putting away anger and wrath, by giving each other grace, and forgiving as Christ forgave us.

Words Have Great Potential

They say that on average women talk three times as much as men. In fact, we speak about 13,000 more words than them each day. An average man will speak 7,000 words while his wife will speak 20,000.[1]

Keep in mind that this is only an average. I probably speak about 60,000 words/day and Michael speaks 10.

Just to give you an idea of how many words that is, the average paperback book has 50,000 words in it. So, if you're an average talker, you'd be filling up half a book all on your own. Every day.

If you've ever read a powerful book, then you know the potential that words have to greatly affect your marriage. Each day is an opportunity for the next chapter to be more powerful and encouraging than the last.

A good book can inspire and motivate you to grow. A good book can be life changing.

Don't Be a Nag

One drip isn't a problem—we all have off days—but a continual drip can cause damage to a relationship when our attitude and our words go unchecked.

It's not easy living with another person. Sometimes complaining feels good but, the thing is, it's *not* good. Loving communication will get us a lot further than nagging ever will.

LOVE LOOKS FOR THE BEST AND HOPES FOR THE BEST IN EACH OTHER.

If we want to be a wife who's an encouragement to her husband, then we need to be exercising that area of our lives.

They Need Our Encouragement

There's a lot of weight on men's shoulders, at least most men I know. When they aren't facing deadlines at work, they're dealing with the spiritual and financial responsibilities that come with leading a family.

And so, while they might appear to have everything under control, most of our husbands would not only appreciate encouragement from us, they would benefit from it.

Author, Matthew L. Jacobson writes, "We need your affirmation—we have to have it and, oh, how we thrive with it. Typically, men are quiet about these things but that doesn't mean we need and enjoy our wife's affirmation any less. And every man feels it: When his woman is behind him, he can slay dragons."

Encouragement is a powerful force. It's the cheer at the end of a race that gives a runner that final push to the finish. It's the nurturing of a parent that instills confidence in their child's life. It's the words of a spouse who inspires you to grow in God's grace.

To encourage someone is to "instill courage" in them. It's more than a compliment, it's a steady reminder that God's on their side, that He is their power and strength, and that all things work out for good to those who are in Christ Jesus.

---

1. *Sorry to Interrupt Dear But Women Really Do Talk More Than Men, by Fiona MacRae Science Correspondent, Mail Online*

Today's Marriage Vow
To Encourage & Edify You

Today's Challenge
Look for ways to encourage your husband today.

Appreciate the Little Things

_____

_____

_____

_____

_____

_____

_____

_____

_____

_____

Dear Heavenly Father,

Your word tells us not to let any unwholesome talk come out of our mouths, but that we should be using our words to encourage each other, and to build each other up.

Help me to respond positively to my husband. Teach me to respect him, and trust him with my heart.

Help me to notice the small things, to realize the many things I take for granted, and to show my appreciation for them.

Help me to look for the best in my husband instead of focusing on his faults. Help me to see him through a veil of compassion and grace the way You do.

Remind me to put in the effort and the energy it takes to please each him more than myself. And may I always seek to please You.

In the name of Jesus, I pray. Amen.

Appendix I

Create a Marriage Mission Statement

Whether we notice or not, we all go into marriage with a goal or two in mind. Whatever that goal or mission is, however, will be different for every couple.

The key is to have the same goal as your husband, and the master key is to have a goal that's focused on the will of the Lord.

A few years ago, when I was setting up my website, a branding expert asked me what my "mission statement" was.

"My mission?" I asked him, "Why do I need a mission?" I wasn't a big company—I was a writer with a blog, so why would I need one?

He went on to tell me that regardless of size a mission statement is a must. It gets you thinking about what's really important to you, and, as the years go by—it helps you stay on track.

As I started looking around, I began to notice, churches have them, big companies have them, small companies have them, bloggers have them... why don't couples?

And then I noticed that my friend Ruth had one for her family, and I absolutely loved the idea of making our own.

Would you like to make one too? If so, get together with your husband, pray about the things you want to include, and have fun putting it together!

Here's a general outline:

1. **Start with a mission.** It can be one line or several. This is ours: "To have a Christ-centered marriage that brings glory to God through the way that we love and the way that we live. That we would be servants of grace who give more than we're given and forgive *before* we're forgiven."

    I encourage you to take this section of your statement and copy it onto a small piece of paper that you can keep out in the open as a constant reminder. If you don't know what to write as your mission, feel free to use the one I have.

2. **List your values.** These are things that are important to you as a couple. For example, they might be things like going to bed together at the same time every night, getting up together every morning, turning the TV off at a certain time, and reading the Bible together every day.

3. **List your goals or dreams.** This could include things like saving for college, retirement, going on a mission trip, setting up a ministry, homeschooling your children, etc. What's interesting about this list is that it can also become a source of prayer for your marriage as you dream about your future together.

The purpose of the mission statement is to keep you focused on those things that are important to your marriage and keep it free from distraction.

Reflect on it often and bring things to prayer if you find that you're veering off track.

Made in the USA
Coppell, TX
22 January 2022